Behind The Glory

Behind The Glory

Birthing Nations

Tiffany Moore

To order additional copies of this book, contact:
Xlibris Corporation
1-888-795-4274
www.Xlibris.com
Orders@Xlibris.com
27579

Contents

To the late Mr. Robert and Mrs. Ella Moore, Mrs. Alice Gilbert, and Mrs. Daisy "Momma Daisy" Jackson. Your legacy will forever live on . . .

Remember Me

Remember me when flowers bloom
Early in the spring
Remember me on sunny days
In the fun that summer brings

Remember me in the fall
As you walk through the leaves of gold
And in the wintertime—remember me
In the stories that are told

But most of all remember
Each day right from the start
I will be forever near
For I live within your heart

—Judith Karen Bulock

Mom and Dad,

There are no words to express how much I love and appreciate you both. I could not ask for better parents.

Dad, you are the epitome of what a father should be. You give your best to ensure that my needs are met. Your love and guidance has inspired me to be a better person.

Mom, you have taught me how to be patient and wait on God. Your unconditional love keeps me going. You have lived a respectable life before me. Thank you for being a virtuous woman.

Thank you both for instilling the love of God in me. You have raised me to work hard and to trust in God. I appreciate the time you have sacrificed to make my life better. I hope that my life is pleasing to you. I will honor you by striving for greater heights in life. You are there through all my failures and success. I pray that God strengthens and keeps your lives so that you may take part in my future endeavors.

I thank God for my parents, Russell and Alice Moore; my brothers, Fletcher, Russell, Jr., Marlon, Joshua, Ezekiel, Ricky, Jacob, Channone, and Cheyenne; and my sisters, Tammy and Crystal. I am grateful for many aunts, uncles, cousins, and my beautiful hometown, Dixon Mills, Alabama. God is blessing me, and I must give him praise. Words cannot express my gratitude for his grace and mercy. I am delighted that he thought so much of me.

Preface

If you are willing and obedient, you shall eat the good of the land. God has done great things for this ministry. Just through two people who were willing and obedient to God's perfect will. Prophetess White set her heart and my heart to write the vision that God gave her. She stepped out on faith, obeyed God, and established ministry. With the love and support of her husband, apostle Richard White, Prophetess Lucinda started the ministry in their five-bedroom home. In spite of what people believed, they trusted God and held services. Many signs and wonders, diverse gifts of the Holy Ghost were performed. It was not long that God opened doors, for them to purchase the sanctuary in Linden, Alabama. Although many spoke that the ministry would not stand because it was led by a woman pastor, God fought for them.

> Except the Lord the build the house; they labor in vain that build it: except the Lord keep the city, the watchman waketh but in vain. (Ps. 127:1)

This book was written to encourage the body of Christ, to trust in God and believe his Word. We must keep our faith and stay on the wall. God wants his people to fight a good fight. My leaders endured much persecution for the

Gospel's sake. I have realized that hardships will come, and they must be met head-on. God said that he will be with us even unto the end of the earth. The leaders taught me how to stay focused and stand on God's promises. People, I adjure you to believe in yourself.

You do not have to hold a title as a pastor, prophet, apostle, or bishop. God's Word declares, "He that believeth on me, as the scripture has said, out of his belly shall flow rivers of living water" (John 7:38). This tells me that anything is possible for them that believe. There is nothing too hard for God! Do not lose your tenacity, determination, and drive.

We are living in an hour where the world is trying to deny God's existence. Therefore, we, as believers in the body of Christ, must pray for one another like never before. We cannot stop calling on Jesus. Persecution is coming, and I assure you, we can stand on Jesus. You can fight a good fight using God's Word. His Word has empowered this ministry to stand. *Behind the Glory* is not about fame and fortune. This book possesses the essence of real warfare. Satan declared that this ministry would come to naught. Moreover, he said, "I will rule." But God fights for us. Since he fights for us, we shall continue to proclaim that Jesus is Lord and Savior of humanity. We must fight for our very existence. Therefore, we encourage you to fight in the Kingdom. God's Word is real, and he will keep his promises. Persecution must come in order for God to be glorified in us. I implore you, readers, do not lose your drive.

Acknowledgments

I thank God, my Lord and Savior. I give honor to my kings, Mr. Russell Moore, Sr., and apostle Richard White; and queens, Mrs. Alice Moore and prophetess Lucinda White. I thank the members of the Firebrands for Christ Ministries International for their prayers, testimonies, and support. I extend my gratitude to my family for their love and support. To the dynamic publishers, producers, reviewers, and others that have dedicated their time and money into making this book a success. I am elated by what God is doing for all of us. Well done!

Chapter 1

Testimonies

Ms. Cheeseburo

I am a miracle. I turned six years old this year. God spoke a word over my life, to live and not die. The doctors told my mother and family that I would be born a breeched baby. First, the doctors confirmed that I was dead in the womb. Then, God turned things around on my behalf. Pastor Richard and copastor Lucinda White prayed over me and commanded my body, soul, and spirit to be revived. Air entered my body as I was in my mother's womb. I weighed less than a pound when I was born. I was immediately taken to the intensive care unit because of my condition and state.

Doctors began to say that I would not live six months. If I survived the surgery, I would be paralyzed. Furthermore, there was a strong possibility that I would be mentally disabled, and Mother would have to nurse me all my life. Doctors spoke and said that I would not last a year, but God spoke a word! God said, "Live."

I attended kindergarten in 2008. I have to study and practice more than my peers, but God's turning that situation around also. I look back and give God the praise. Truly he is real. When I entered into his house, I ran around the sanctuary clapping my hands and singing praises because God saved me. I was dead, and now I live. I enjoy music, shopping, T-ball, eating, and being with my grandmother (Prophetess Parker), who has stood by my side and helped raise me.

Prophetess Jackson

Where do I begin? God has always looked out for me. Ever since I was a little girl, he was there by my side. I have so much to thank God for. He blessed me with a praying mother that held me up. Furthermore, he saved and raised my sister, prophetess Lucinda White. I do not know where I would be without my sister.

I have almost been in a mental institution. I have died so many times. I fight demons from hell every night. He was there through it all. I can testify that God is a healer. I have suffered from diabetes, hypothyroidism, and asthma. Through all my sickness and disease, God heals me every day. I am miracle, and God gets the glory. I praise him for being my way-out of no way-out, a best friend, and the strength of my life. I thank God for the Word, which states, "No weapon formed against me shall prosper." Through it all, I "look unto the hills from which cometh my help, all of my help cometh from God."

People, you got to know that God is on your side. I have gone through a divorce and almost lost my children. I didn't have a job at the time, and I was left homeless. I went through hell and suffered much. Then I had to forgive those that hurt me and cast my name out for evil. I began to ask God, "Lord, how much more must I take?" As I cried unto him, God changed my situation around. He healed my body and heart. God blessed me with a nice home and transportation. I look back and see that God made a lie out of the devil. My faith has gone to another level, and I believe God for anything. He didn't let me go down. I am a single mother, and God pays my bills. I don't want for nothing.

To women out there who thinks no one cares and you are alone, I encourage you to hold on. When it seems like your situations won't work out, remember God is a provider. He sees your circumstances. Hold on to God!

Prophet Jackson

God made me a prophet for this last hour to preach an expectable year of the Lord. I thank God for realness. My life was headed for destruction when God called my name. I thank God for my mother. She was a wise, praying woman. I am grateful for my sister and brother-in-law, Apostle Richard and prophetess Lucinda White. Lastly, I appreciate the love of my life, Mrs. Jackson.

People of God, I can testify that God is a healer, savior, deliverer, and whatever you need him to be. Before I received the baptism of the Holy Ghost, I had three bad demons to defeat in my life. Gambling, drinking, and smoking were the three bad demons that had a contract on my life. In addition, Satan decreed that I was not going to amount to anything. I was headed to a speedy death. All I can say is "Look at me now."

Not only that, I had a bad marriage. My first wife led two lives; she did not want the things of God. I went through hell because I loved her and refused to get a divorce. But I did not know God had a plan for my life. He wanted me power packed and Holy Ghost—filled.

People say prophets go through some strange things. I cannot share all of what God has done, but he intervened in the nick of time. I can testify that he raised a woman that loves him. She is my soul mate and the mother of my children. I encourage those that are married to stay before God and work together. The devil desires to destroy the men and women of God. It is imperative that you support each other, communicate, and stay unified. Remember no weapon that forms against you shall prosper.

Mrs. Richardson

This testimony is how I met God and came to know him. I have no regrets. Back in August 1994, I began to get sick in my body. First, it started in my stomach; everything I ate came right out. Then in my throat, it felt like something was in it, so I went to the doctor. He gave me medication that did not work. Next, my head started bothering me. It felt like things were crawling inside my head. The crawling would start while I was sleeping. So I went back to the doctor. He prescribed Xanax (nerve pills). I also received a shot, and the medication did not work. My illness only worsened, and I became terrified. My doctor referred me to an ear, throat, and nose specialist. The physicians took x-rays, and everything seemed normal. I went to see a heart specialist, and my entire test came back fine. Finally, I received an x-ray on my head to look for tumors or any burst blood vessels.

I quickly became irritated. I began to say to myself, "I hope that something is found because I am tired of tests and not improving in my health." After those tests came back negative, I changed doctors. These doctors did not find anything wrong with me. My family members were seriously worried because my health was not improving. I lost a large amount of weight, and my complexion was very dark.

One day, I was approached by a lady, and she suggested that someone had used witchcraft on me. She said that she could help. She took me to a man that gave some instructions to follow. I told my mother that this man is the devil and threw everything in the garbage.

I thank God for this pastor that prayed for me. She told my cousin to bring me back to their service. On that day, I heard voices telling me that I was not going to make it and that I would die. During the service, the pastor said that they had been fasting and praying for me. She also gave me Luke 13:17 to read. Then she told me to come in front of the church. They all began to surround me and anoint me with oil. As they prayed, the pastor began to command the spirits to come out in Jesus's name. My cousin said that she saw my face light up. My complexion was not dark anymore. God had healed me that night. And before I could get out of the parking lot, I was fast asleep. I had not slept in over three months. I was not sick anymore.

The pastor told me that God had something that he wanted me to do. He was going to come to me in my dreams and let me know. After months went by, I went back to my old sins. The next year, during the Fourth of July in Linden, a tent was put up near my house. I attended the service that Friday night. That night, Evangelist White (Prophetess White) at the time was the speaker for the hour. She was preaching about shacking up and fornication, and I have not heard anybody like her before. I was amazed at the people falling down and shaking on the ground. I was afraid because it was all new to me. I did not return the following night, but I sent my children instead. The following night, I received a message from the people that I should attend the next service. I got in the prayer line that night. Prophetess White asked me I wanted the Holy Ghost. She said, "I see you are not able to sleep." She said that God was dealing with me.

I began to go to their church and attend Monday-night prayer wheel. I began to seek God for the Holy Ghost. I was calling on Jesus and still shacking up. Finally, I decided that I was not going to fornicate anymore. In September 1995, I told my friend, who is my husband today, that I could not live like this because I wanted the Holy Ghost. One night, on my couch as I was asleep, I heard a voice say to me, "It's holiness or hell." From that point on, I began to run for my life.

In October 1995, God filled me with the precious gift of the Holy Ghost. That night I said to myself, "I do not care who is looking at me." I just called on the name of Jesus. I did not fall out; I just started speaking in tongue. And I knew I had received the Holy Ghost.

I got married two months later. And give God all the glory and honor in Jesus's name.

Dr. Moore

I was diagnosed with lupus in 1996. Since then I have battled my body, mind, and spirit. Lupus attacks the auto immune system (the body fights against itself). My white (T cells) blood count was extremely high, and instead of attacking the disease and infections, the white blood cells attacked the body, which resulted in me having arthritis and other complications. I have experienced skin breakouts, hair loss, kidney problems, liver problems, and much more. Every day has been a struggle, but God heals me daily. My joints ached from inflammation buildup, and my muscles contracted, which prevented me from carrying out basic tasks. Since I have been under the Word of God in this ministry, God healed me. When I look back over my life and see what God did for me, my soul just begins to weep. I know I could not have survived without him. Prayer has kept and healed me. From 1996 until now, my life has been an uphill journey. God did it for me.

Many years ago I wanted to be a doctor, pediatrician to be exact. I wanted to work with children. That was my goal all through high school and undergraduate. One year before receiving my undergraduate degree, I gave my life to God. What now? I must dedicate as much time to God as possible. I was baptized with the Holy Ghost the same night I met Prophetess White. God gave me a strong love for her and the ministry. I could not explain any of it. Everything was so new. I was dressed very ridiculously that Friday night. I realized no one had on earrings, no makeup, skirts down to the floor, arms covered to the wrist, and collars up to the necks. The women had their hair in ponytails and bangs. As crazy as this was, I wanted to be a part of it. I was saved on April 21, 2000, that Friday night. I had to get to that woman's church.

Before going back to school, I attended Prophetess White's church. My mother and I attended that Sunday. When I went to the church on Sunday, God instantly gave me a connection with her spirit. I needed to talk to her. I went to school on Sunday evening and called her all week. I got rid of my pants, jewelry, and everything. They were in tradition at that time, so I had to become as they were. I did not question anything Prophetess White said. She knew every problem, spirit, and demon I was dealing with. I wanted to be saved for real. I had a desire to be saved no matter what the cost.

Ministry means everything to me. Now why am I questioning myself on whether or not I heard God on my purpose for being where I am now? Jesus gave his all for me. Why could I not continue on my present journey without worry? I have endured much opposition in my life. Ridicule from friends, talked about behind my back, and misunderstood by my family was all worth it. There is no explanation to why I love God and this ministry so much that I would drive four to five hours to attend church every Sunday.

I moved back home after achieving a chiropractic doctorial degree from Life University in 2005. My dreams were about to be fulfilled when my sickness made a turn for the worst. It was during a seminar that I became ill.

Although the lupus was out of control, I remained at the seminar. While there, I realized that my sickness would forever torment me. I began to compare myself to the others around me. One older gentleman informed me that he had been in business for over forty years. Another chiropractor said that he had practiced for at least twenty-three years, and his business was growing. He shared that it would be hard at first, but things would improve. I quickly removed myself from their company because I felt out of place. Then I questioned my purpose and calling during that point in life. Did I really hear from God when he led me to move back home? Why was my condition in this state? With all the knowledge that I have, I cannot take care of myself. I am basically dependent on my parents. To make matters worse, I did not know how my dreams would be accomplished.

Battling with lupus, not practicing in my career field, enduring hardships, living with my parents, and depending on God has been my process. God did not tell me I had to go through this process to get to my expected end. Many times I wanted to give up and throw in the towel because trials got so hard. I had no job, no money, nowhere to live, and a deadly disease that was out of control.

If it is destiny, it will come to pass. Even if it takes ten or twenty years, wait on God. He will fulfill his promises. The kingdom of heaven suffers violence; the violent take by force. I realized that the tests I underwent had nothing to do with me. God had a plan for my life. God had the plan, not "Tammy." It's all about God and what he has in store for my life. It did not and still does not feel good when you go through tests for Jesus' sake. I encouraged myself because the struggles are for the Kingdom and the ministry.

Prophetess Parker

You name it, I did it! But I am here because of the grace of God. I don't have a college degree, but I am intelligent and full of the Holy Ghost. I am on the Lord's side now, and everything is all right. No weapon that forms against me shall prosper. I am the righteousness of God. I have not seen the righteous forsaken nor his seed begging bread. I come to testify that when

God is for you, then he is more than the whole world against you. I'm here to testify that God won't let you go down. God is right there when your family and your own children turn their backs.

We are in our finest hour. For those individuals that have been faithful, God is getting ready to pour out his spirit on us. We are about to inherit many blessings. Miracles, signs, and wonders are about to take place in the earth. I charge the single women to get hold of God like never before. Yes, I see the hurt and pain, but God is your provider. He is your strength.

I am a prophetess of the Lord, and the devil hates me. He tried to kill me many times. He had contracts out to stop the move of God in my life. Satan declared that I would remain a whore and will not reach my destiny. Growing up, I knew God had his hands on me. I was a liar and a thief. I loved money and sex. I went from man to man. I married against God and my pastor's wishes. I went through hell in that marriage. Because of disobedience to God and my leaders, I suffered in my body. I was hemorrhaging and losing a lot of blood. The doctors told me that I must undergo three major operations. But God had mercy on me and used Prophetess White to heal me.

God also used the prophetess to rebuke and chasten me. I often got mad and wanted to leave the church. However, God commanded me to stay there, take the rebuke, and undergird the ministry. As I went through my process, I saw God turn my life around. I can now move and operate in the things of God because my spirit is right. Under this ministry, God has taught me how to be faithful and obedient. His Word declared in Isaiah 1:19 that "if you are willing and obedient, you will eat the good of the Land."

I watched God heal my grandbaby. He brought my daughter from death's door, and God keeps saving my son. God promised me that he will not let me go down. God said he will keep me if I served him. I encourage you to go through your process. This is my testimony of how I came to know God and receive the Holy Ghost. I have no regrets because I love him. God gets the glory and the honor for my life.

Chapter 2

What Manner of Church Is This?

The Firebrands for Christ Ministries International

Tried in the fire and we come out as pure gold! God resides at this house. Even as John spoke to the Seven Churches of Asia, God is speaking to this church today. Set your house in order. Whatever you are going to do for God, do it quickly. People, God is soon to come. Will you be ready?

This is a glimpse of what our ministry has and must continue to undergo for his name's sake. The very gates of hell rose up, but did not prevail. God has his hands on us. So we pressed toward the mark and looked to Christ Jesus, "the author and finisher of our faith" (Heb. 12:2). Surely, "no weapon formed against us shall prosper and every tongue that shall rise up in judgment thou shall be condemn" (Isa. 54:17). If God be for us, he is more than the whole world against us. We greet you in the name of Jesus.

Tell me! What manner of church is this? A revival is coming to America. A trumpet is about to sound, and God is going to put Linden on the map. It is not about how *big* your church is. How *big* God is! We went beyond what we did not see. It is all about what God is doing. God said, "Stop thinking small." Our mind-set has changed; you got to get out of the box. We serve a big God. See beyond your normal circumstances. You cannot focus on your money. God has given us favor, favor with him and man. We waited on God to perform his Word. He watches over his word, and he hastens to perform it. God is about to dumbfound this city, state, and nations. We have to keep our mouths closed and watch God move. In the midst of persecution, we have to hold our peace and give God praise. We praise him because we are expecting God to do just what he said. Can you feel that something is about to happen? The supernatural, that unusual miracle, is coming forth in this hour. What the devil said would not happen—would not have happened. Don't settle for the mediocre.

The new church is coming forth, the church with power and having the power to stand to declare that Jesus is alive. This church, FFC Ministries International, is built upon prayer and order. We are operating in the spirit of excellence. The leaders carry revival in their bellies. We are pressing to that rim in God where nothing will forsake our faith. When you come to the FFC ministry, come with great expectations. Everything that you need, God has it in this ministry. It is at 603 Abbott Street, where the feast of the Lord is going on!

Habakkuk 1:5 says, "Behold ye among the heathen, and regard, and wonder marvelously: for I will work a work in your days which ye will not believe, though it be told you." Yes, God is up to something, and it is marvelous in our eyes. Though it be told you, God ordained Apostle Richard and Prophetess Lucinda White for such a time as this to proclaim the Gospel of Jesus Christ. The apostle and prophetess house a fivefold ministry. Though it is told to you, many still will not believe. God has done the supernatural within the ministry. He raised it up in just a few years. The ministry has grown internationally. God said that it shall go worldwide spiritually and naturally. Isaiah 1:19 says, "If you are willing and obedient, you shall eat the good of the land." The Word also teaches that "the meek shall inherit the earth."

We thank God for what has taken place. God is adding daily, those that should be saved, to the church. Many may wonder about the name of this ministry. Why not COGIC of Linden, Pentecostal Faith No. 5, or Primitive

Baptist of Linden? Neither the bishop nor the grant fellowship foundation can get recognition for the ministry because to God the glory belongs. Firebrands for Christ was given because God would send people who have been through the fires of life. God is literally plucking out souls that many people have cast away from the hands of Satan. God is saving people that have been abused and trampled over by society. Firebrands are able to stand the storm. They get stronger when they are tested.

God has established this ministry to provide life to a dying people.

> And the Lord said unto Satan, The Lord rebuke thee, O Satan; even the Lord that has chosen Jerusalem rebuke thee: is not this a brand plucked out of the fire? Now Joshua was clothed with filthy garments and stood before the angel. And he answered and spoke unto those that stood before him, saying take away the filthy garments from him. (Zech. 3:2-4)

Satan has destroyed many souls. God is sending them from north, south, east, and west. Miracles are taking place. Blinded eyes are being opened. Deaf ears are being unstopped. Diverse gifts of the Holy Ghost are yet performed. Have you been plucked out of the fire? Has God redeemed your soul? We have witnessed the move of God's spirit. The anointing of God rests and dwells at FFC Ministries International.

Chapter 3

History

We shall live and not die to declare the works of the Lord. This is just a glimpse of what God has done in the FFC ministry. We count it all joy. For we know that this ministry is blessed by God himself. No man will ever get the glory. The glory belongs to God. Our faith has been tested and proven many times before. We write unto you to show forth what God can do with a people. Our journey has only begun. Although God has something great waiting, our story still has not been told. The Word of God teaches in Zechariah 4:6 that it is "not by power or by might, but by my Spirit says the Lord." God is truly up to something.

Our eyes have not seen nor have our ears heard, neither has it entered into the hearts of men the things that God has in store for his people (1 Cor. 2:9).

The FFC ministry was established and founded in October 11, 1999, under the leadership of Apostle Richard and Prophetess Lucinda White. The church is located at 603 Abbott Street in Linden, Alabama. The Lord specifically told Pastor White to name it the Firebrands for Christ because he would send people that had been plucked out of the burning.

After serving eight years faithfully in ministry at her previous church, God called Lucinda out to lead. In a society where many believed women should not preach, pastor, or even be in the pulpit, Prophetess White tuned in and set her heart and hearing only unto the voice of God. Years earlier, God had already assured Prophetess White that whenever she would step out and obey him, signs and wonders would forever follow the ministry. Two signs would be that the ministry would consist of people coming from the north, south, east, and west; whatever endeavors that this team undertook, God's blessings would be upon them (prospering everything they touched). Excluding the members in the local area, many drive at least one to four hours every Sunday and sometimes during the week to attend their services.

FFC Ministries International held its first dedication service in January 2000. In January 2002, the ministry completed an expansion work of the sanctuary to accommodate God's end-time harvest. The expansion has been completed, and there are several ministries under the ministry's umbrella.

Chapter 4

Visions and Dreams

I will stand upon my watch, and set me upon the tower, and will watch to see what he will say unto me, and what I shall answer when I am reproved. And the Lord answered me, and said, Write the vision, and make it plain upon tables, that he may run that readeth it. For the vision is yet for an appointed time, but at the end it shall speak, and not lie: though it tarry, wait for it; because it will surely come, it will not tarry.

—Habakkuk 2:1-3

As God raised the prophets of old and schooled them, God himself has raised Lucinda and Richard White for such a time as this. Surely, her answer was yes to what God had given her. Prophetess White made a vow to God that she will not let his name go down. "Eyes have not seen, ears have not heard, neither has it entered into the heart of man the things God has for his people."

What you are about to read in this chapter will change your life forever. There are many prophets, apostles, teachers, pastors, and others that have been used by God. However, at this point in time, White is on the scene. God himself is about to walk the earth through her and men, women, boys, and girls shall be delivered. People are coming out of captivity and bondage. Governments systems will be changed. A decree has been made, and God is going to fight for his people. The chapter is entitled "Visions and Dreams" because the prophet has dreamed about the end-time church for many years. Now God is about to prove to this generation about who he really is. As you read this chapter, allow God to minister to you concerning your purpose in the earth. The first thing the prophetess desires to share with you is about her assignment on the earth.

The Outer-Body Experience

In 1991, God sent me into the woods to process me for destiny. About five years ago, while I was on my face praying, drunken in the presence of the Lord, I encountered one of many outer-body experiences. I felt my spirit lift up out of my body as though it was an airplane taking off of the runway. I felt myself going higher and then leveling out like a 747. The first place that God took me was down by the woods where he processed and had me praying for over fourteen years. He then allowed me to fly from corner to corner of the United States of America, naming out cities and states as I passed over them. He then took me across many waters flying across international soil naming out various countries. Upon the conclusion of the flight, I felt my spirit lowering itself as a plane descends to the ground. He then very vividly spoke these words, "My daughter, for I would say unto thee, get ready to mount up with wings as an eagle. You will go throughout this earth bringing great deliverance unto the people. I will use you to execute judgment and righteousness in the earth, and your voice will draw millions unto me. Your voice will be heard and will become a voice that will sit upon many waters. Because you paid the price, I will allow no man to get the glory out of your life. I will be glorified within you. I will get the glory, because it is due me."

Dream

In the year of 2005, God came unto me while my head was upon my pillow. I was standing upon a platform that was very large and long. I held a microphone to my lips, and as I looked down preaching, lo and behold, it was a field filled with white sheep. It was one of the most beautiful sights that I had ever witnessed. The sheep were all baaing with heads lifted toward me in attentive mode. As far as my eyes could see, there were sheep touching sheep everywhere. They were knitted so close together that I could not even see the grass in the field. Each time I would lift my hands to reverence and glorify the Almighty, the sheep, in unison, would make obeisance. So I began to walk down these steps to be in their midst. Because they were so great, I spoke and told God, "I can't do this alone, Lord, I need help." As I turned my head around and about, my husband, Richard, stood on the right and my brother, Leo, stood on the left. As I began making a straight path through the sheep, they began clearing the aisle for me to pass through.

When I finally reached the end of the field, I came to a building surrounded by many satellites, huge and small. As I proceeded to go up these steps, there was a woman at the top awaiting me, holding the door wide open. As I neared the door to enter in, the woman was prophetess Juanita Bynum. She led me into this room to sit on this couch. Shortly afterward, Brother Paul and Jan Crouch and others entered into the room. They all began embracing me with the love of Christ. Jan began to weep as she looked upon me and said, "I see Jesus, I see Jesus, I see Jesus." They then began pushing me into the fullness of time. The pushed me into destiny.

Prophetess White

We bless God for the vision that he has placed on the inside of the prophetess. Many lives have already been touched through her life. God took the prophetess worldwide on October 23, 2005. Just like all the visions and dreams that had shown Prophetess Lucinda, Prophetess Bynum opened the door for her to be on TBN. During the *Praise the Lord* broadcast, Prophetess Bynum introduced Lucinda White to the world. On this particular broadcast, Prophetess White shared a portion of a testimony about her wilderness experience. Not only was the prophetess there to give a testimony to the world, Lucinda White made a bold statement saying, "I was sent by God to give you Prophetess Bynum an impartation from the woods." Since that time, prophetess Lucinda White became known as the Woods Lady. All the visions and dreams began to come to pass. God did just what he said. There are other visions and dreams to be shared by the woman concerning destiny. You can read about them in the prophetess's upcoming personal books that she will write as God leads her.

> Write the vision, and make it plain upon tables that he may run that readeth it. For the vision is yet for an appointed time, but at the end it shall speak, and not lie. Though it tarry, wait for it; because it will surely come, it will not tarry. (Hab. 2:2-3)

Chapter 5

Transition

This chapter deals with the transitions that God took pastor Lucinda White through. Many know that she is more than a pastor. She is also a prophet of the Lord. God released Pastor White into her destiny of walking in the office of a prophet. God also ordained her husband, apostle Richard White, to be the pastor in this hour. What you are about to read was supernaturally given to me by the Holy Ghost. Prophetess White's spirit and God visited me one night in my bedroom. I was writing some things down that God had already showed me in the spirit. Then I began to hear the pastor's voice so clearly.

Called to Nations

There is always a great trial that comes to get you off course when God is getting ready to elevate you. It is called transition. Transition comes in the most awkward times in our lives. Mainly, when things are going well, and to us, it seems like everything is falling in place. The perfect plans we call them. God is really blessing, we say. And sometimes he does allow us to complete or walk through some tasks. You know how it is. We begin to prosper by our own knowledge and wisdom. Everyone is there to support what you are doing. Sometimes we become bored with what we are doing, but we won't admit to it. We won't admit to being bored because it is working for us.

The level where we are has caused some frustrations, and we become angry, restless, and stressed out. The vision has enlarged itself on the inside of you. Not only has it enlarged itself, the people around you become annoying. Nothing can satisfy you where you are in this level anymore. Fear has taken control now. *I can't leave this establishment*, you tell yourself over and over again. You begin to hate going to work or anything now. Why? God is calling you to another platform. You can't understand what is going on inside of you. Transition is taking place, and, God, how can I accept what you are doing?

For me, transition happened in a matter of weeks. I did not have time to think about what I was leaving. Nor did I have time to think about where I was going. All I had was a word from God. There was something in my spirit that drove me to my next level. I was not comfortable where I was. Then God came and called my name. He forced me to pray just a little longer and harder. The platform where God had taken me brought on a lot of pain. Many, many nights and days I would cry and truly did not know why. All I had was a word from God. The platform where God had taking me caused many people to turn on me. My name was cast aside for no reasons at all. My name and reputation were destroyed by my foes and enemies. Thank God for transition because you find out who your true friends are.

Through it all, I remained focused on what God had promised. I knew that God would use me to do mighty exploits, but there was a part of me that did not want to take on such a burden. God had to kill my flesh. To take on nations was not an easy assignment. But I told God yes. I told God that I will not let his name go down. I told God that I will go if it costs my life. Transition was not easy, but I thank God that it came so that men, women, boys, and girls may know him.

People, you don't understand the price that was paid for the anointing that is resting in my life. God took me on the back side of the desert for such a time as this. That's why I keep myself unspotted from the world. For it is no longer I that live, but Christ. If I never preached another ceremony, I want to be saved. Glory be to God! I want to be saved. I love people, but I won't let you make a god out me. I won't let you prostitute this anointing. For as I stand this day to declare warfare on the devil's head. God's will be done in my life. "Heyeee!" I say. God's will be done in my life!

Many of you may only know me as the Woods Lady, but if I never greet or set my eyes upon you, I love you and mean Jesus all the way.

I thank God for what he has placed on the inside. To my beloved husband, apostle Richard White, carry the vision on and be very much encouraged.

God not only allowed Prophetess White's spirit to visit and minister to me, he took me in the Bible and gave specific scriptures that pertain to her life. The following scriptures mostly describe her assignment in the earth.

The Mission of God's Servant

> Behold my servant, whom I uphold; Mine elect, in whom my soul delighteth; I have put my spirit upon him: He shall bring forth judgment to the Gentiles. He shall not cry, nor lift up, Nor cause his voice to be heard in the street. A bruised reed shall he not break, And the smoking flax shall he not quench: He shall bring forth judgment unto truth. He shall not fail nor be discouraged, until he have set judgment in the earth: And the isles shall wait for his law. Thus saith God the Lord, He that created the heavens, and stretched them out; He that spread forth the earth, and that which cometh out of it; He that breath unto the people upon it, And spirit to them to walk therein: I the Lord have called thee in righteousness, And will hold thine hand and will keep thee, And give thee for a covenant of the people, for a light of the Gentiles; To open blind eyes, To bring out the prisoners from the prison, And them that sit in darkness out of the prison house. I am the Lord: that is my name: And my glory will I not give to another, Neither my praise to graven images. Behold, the former things are come to pass, And new things do I declare: Before they spring forth I tell you of them. (Isa. 42:1-9)

As Isaiah cried and pleaded with the people in his day, prophetess Lucinda White is making a cry in the earth, compelling the people to return back to God.

The Servant's Call

> Listen, O isles, unto me; And hearken, ye people from afar; The Lord hath called me from the womb, From the bowels of my mother hath he made mention of my name. And he hath made my mouth like a sharp sword; In the shadow of his hand hath he hid me, And made me a polished shaft; In his quiver hath he hid me; And said unto me, Thou art my servant, O Israel, in whom I will be glorified. Then I said, I have labored in vain, I have spent my strength for naught, and in vain: Yet surely my judgment is with the Lord, And my work with my God. And now, saith the Lord that formed me from the womb to be his servant, To bring Jacob again to him, Though Israel be not gathered, Yet shall I be glorious in the eyes of the Lord, And my God shall be my strength. And he said, it is a light thing that thou should be my servant Jacob, And to restore the preserved of Israel: I will also give thee for a light to the Gentiles, That thou may be my salvation unto the end of the earth. (Isa. 49:1-6)

During our time of transition, we experienced great hardship. Our leaders were tested on every hand. For those leaders that were preaching the unadulterated Gospel of Jesus Christ, you will be tried on every hand. Why? Satan desires to destroy your ministry. He has contracts out for FFC to stop the move of God. But God brings the ministry out. Satan often speaks and decrees that the ministry will not stand.

We believe the report of the Lord. If he be for us, he is more than the whole world against us. God fights our battles, and he is well able to deliver us from the hand of Satan. We are experiencing the death of loved ones. Many of us are losing everything for the ministry. Family members and friends are walking away. God is testing our faith and loyalty to him. In addition, we believe God wants to show us ourselves. We are in our wilderness experience and giving God the glory.

His Word declares in Matthew 19:29, "And everyone that has forsaken houses, or brethren, or sister, or father, or mother, or wife, or children, or lands, for my name's sake, shall receive a hundredfold, and shall inherit everlasting life." Because we are being faithful to ministry, God is about to double and triple our blessings.

For those that survive their wilderness experience, God is about to reward you. There are some hidden things God has for you. I encourage you to stay faithful and obedient to God and your leaders. After you complete your Passover, God has an anointing waiting for you.

Pastors and other leaders, when God brings you into your wealthy place, you will appreciate the warfare and fiery trials that great ministries go through. Stay faithful and obedient to God in your trials. God is coming to your rescue; he is coming when you are truly prepared to receive your inheritance. There are some of you that have not been faithful to the ministry and God. It is in your best interest to become faithful. Undergird your leaders in prayer, fasting, and of course, your finances.

The best times to uplift your leaders and the ministry are when they experience hardships. Remember that Jesus needed his disciples, and they forsook him. That lesson is for our learning. We should not forsake ministry when times are difficult. We praise God and celebrate our leaders when things are going well in our lives and the ministry is prospering. What about the dark days in life? We must trust God the more to deliver. God comes to our rescue when we cry out to him.

Chapter 6

The Enemy Within

For many are called, but few are chosen. How can one like Pastor and Apostle White do the works that they have done unless God be with them? A mighty move of God has taken place through their lives. Is it that God has spoken to a nation of people himself? How can this be? Two humble people that God himself placed in the earth. Signs and wonders have taken place in the earth. The high priest in the Kingdom, yet the apostle and the pastor walk through the earth, and men won't receive them because their hearts have strayed away. Truly, in the last days, men won't receive sound doctrine, but they will have itching ears. They will turn their ear away from truth and shall be turned unto fables.

It is written that a prophet is without honor except in his own country. The man and woman of God have labored many excruciating years in an area where the people only hardened their hearts and turned a deaf ear. Many miracles were not performed because of the unbelief of the people. Yet and still, the pastor and the apostle stood in God's stead for the people. A people of who turned their backs on God's people. Many of the traitors were within the FFC's ministry. In addition, the congregation hindered the flow of God for many years.

What do you do when you can't trust your own people? It is amazing how people enter the house of God and pretend like they are so holy and sanctified. The people praised God, worshipped, rolled over the floor, spoke in tongues, but hated God's anointed one. The leaders warred among one another. No one wanted to obey leadership. We say we love God, but we hate our sister and brother without a cause. Everybody wanted somebody to blame. But did anyone get alone with God?

Nevertheless, the apostle and pastor rolled up their sleeves and chose to deliver God's people for real. No matter what demonic force came against the ministry, God himself fought on their behalf: jealousy, pride, whoredom, witchcraft, backbiting, murder, hatred, hypocrisy, adultery, uncleanness, fornication, variance, emulations, homosexuality, envy, revelry, and the like. The very gates of hell came, but did not prevail.

Thank God for his Word. Through it all, God used the man and woman of God to cut down and uproot all the hell out of the people. The more we were disobedient, the harder they preached. Many did walk away from the ministry. But for everyone that walked away, God sent two, five, and ten more. God said, "That for every one that left, would have to return, for the apostle and pastor to deliver them." Not only that, God himself would send people from all over the world to the ministry—a people with the vision already on the inside, and people hungry for God. This Church of Jesus Christ of Latter-Day Saints that God is raising up won't give the pastor and leaders a hard time. The later church will walk in the anointing and power of God. From 2006 to 2008, the church was tested at every level. The word came through the prophetess that God was no longer going to shake the earth but heaven also. The first things tested were our faith, loyalty, and obedience. You must understand that "the enemy comes to kill, steal and to destroy. But I come that you might have life and that more abundantly" (John 10:10). Satan had a plan to destroy the faithful ones, but we were strengthened in the Word of God. In our season of warfare, we were faced with one trial after another. God allowed us to be proven in our trials. We learned how to labor in prayer and fasting.

Chapter 7

Deliverance

Man cannot live by bread alone, but by every word that proceeded out from God. Even before she started the Firebrands for Christ Ministries in 1999, God gave the prophetess a burden for souls. God established the apostle and the prophetess in the earth to win an end-time harvest into the kingdom of heaven. All the prophetess had was a word from God that she would lead a people. The prophetess was not only going to lead a people, God would use her to birth nations of peoples. As the pastor of Firebrands for Christ Ministries, Prophetess White had to encounter many things. Once she realized what God was doing for her and her husband's ministry, Prophetess White encouraged the congregation to grab the horns of the altar. The task was not an easy one. How could she condition the people to receive what God was doing? Traditions had to be broken off the people. God wanted his people's mind to come out of Egypt. Many members fought against the change in the ministry. The congregation still had the residue of the old church on it. The congregation's mind-set was not spiritual. The people wanted to remain in their comfort zone. There were some who doubted the leader's vision. No matter how much God did through the pastor and prophetess, many members still chose to be disobedient.

The Firebrands for Christ Ministries first started out as the "traditional" holiness or Pentecostal church. The congregation had no idea that God was taking its leaders through transition. This transition took place in order for the apostle and prophetess to receive an end-time harvest. The congregation's mind-set was still at the old church spiritually. It was accustomed to the traditional dress appearance and lifestyle that was taught for some many years. It can be called the religion of clothing. The congregation still had the judgmental and hypocritical spirit. For so long the holiness churches have doomed people to hell because of their lifestyle and or attire. God had to first break the judgmental spirit of the leaders.

In the year of 2004, God began to speak through the mouths of many prophets. The prophets would all say the same things: line upon line and precept upon precept. Then our leaders would take the platform before the people and confess what God was doing. Holiness is still right; our leaders would always remind us. However, the heart of man is what God was truly looking at. God began to let the apostle and prophetess see through the eyes of Jesus. The prophetess knew that God would place her before many notable people. Prophetess White began to go after God with a passion. Prophetess White encouraged herself in the Lord. God began to visit her and the apostle in a mighty way. There were many services where the leaders would mount the platform and deliver a fresh word from heaven. Destiny was calling the prophetess to take her place in earth. God began to speak in the services, and miracles began to take place. More and more prophets from all over the world were calling the leaders and encouraging them to stay focused.

Although fought by the congregation and community, the prophetess did not let anything hinder her walk with God. Many people began to walk away from God and the ministry. The leaders began to face demonic forces from hell like never before. Many of the spirits were brought by the members within the church. The more forces came, the harder the leaders preached to deliver God's people. God began to remove people from the church. The trials came to not only test the leaders, but to test the people of God as well. God began to rebuke like never before. The members soon realized that the vision was going to be accomplished with or without them. The members began to see that God was chastening the congregation for its sins. The fault was not in the leaders; it was in the people. The people wanted to hinder the work. It was the congregation who refused to seek God for the vision of the house.

The preachers, teachers, ushers, praise team, dance team, choir members, and armor bearers all had to seek God for deliverance. God began to reestablish order within the church. God is not going to let the apostle and prophetess be brought to an open shame. God himself began to deal with the people. Traditions began to break off the people. The leaders encouraged the congregations to seek God for the love of him and the ministry.

In the year of 2005, the congregation began to focus on ministry. It realized that it had already lost too much time because of disobedience. Although deliverance was taking place within the hearts of the people, the enemy still showed its head. The apostle and prophetess had to kill out many other forces that wanted to destroy the people of God. Jealousy, backbiting, gossip, lying, manipulation, fornication, disobedience, pride, hate, and controlling spirits had to be cast out of the people. God called for a solemn assembly. He called for a revival within the church. This was not any ordinary revival. This revival was held so God's people would have one last time to come clean. In this particular revival, God placed fire on the altar. The revival was entitled "a Purging Revival." God purged out all the hell that remained in the people. This revival took place to deliver those who wanted to be free from sin. God began to dig out the residue that the people wanted to hold on to. The anointing was so strong in the place. No one left the same way they came. This particular revival also placed the people in the place that they could hear from God. God had mercy on the people. His mercy was poured out on the people like never before.

After the revival, the leaders totally focused on destiny. No longer did the leaders worry about the people that wanted to do what they wanted to. The members began to see a different side of the leaders. The prophetess began to mount the pulpit and declare the Word of the Lord like never before. There was a season where God completely separated her from the people. The prophetess would go into the wilderness and seek God for days. She began to shut herself in her home with God. God brought her in a place with him where nothing would shake her faith. Not only did God put the leaders in a place, God began to establish the faithful members as well.

The congregation began to push the leaders like never before. God placed a love for ministry inside of the people. Once the members got their minds off their situation and focused on the ministry's needs, God began to drop mantles on the lay members. God began to anoint different people for certain tasks in the Kingdom. The congregation realized it had to mature.

Unity is now being established in the ministry, and the people are pulling together to work the vision of the house. The congregation is seeking God for its destiny. We are giving into the leaders' bosoms.

God's Word does not lie. If God said it, he will make it good. I, the author, encourage the readers to support your leaders in what God has given them. One thing that we have learned in the FFC's ministry is that we are not above our leaders. We are learning that God only respects obedience. Being faithful to leadership is the key. Obeying those that have rule over us is what will keep us out of sin. Your degrees and knowledge cannot measure up to your leaders. Just like God spoke to Moses face-to-face, he does the same for our leaders. The ministry has many offices and departments within it. We are a gifted and educated congregation, but our knowledge and talents do not measure up to our leaders. Like Paul, we count these gifts and knowledge lost to gain Christ. When we humble ourselves and acknowledge the God in our leaders, things begin to change for the better in our lives. There are so many testimonies to be shared, but books could not hold them. God moves for us when we put the leader's needs ahead of our own. It sounds crazy, but we cannot deny the miracles and blessings that are being received. The favor of God has been resting in my life since I joined the ministry. If the readers desire to learn anything from this book, obedience is the key. One must be faithful to ministry. I did not get anointed by preaching, teaching, dancing, or singing. I did not get anointed by healing the sick or casting out devils. God said that I was able to do those things because I was a believer. I got anointed by God from being faithful, obedient, and serving God's people.

As the saints of God, we must learn to take rebuke and correction. Since I have been in the ministry, I witnessed people miss what God had for them because they did not want to obey leadership. They could not take corrections because they wanted to know more than the pastor.

If you find yourself getting mad at your leaders and others for telling you the truth, I encourage you to check your spirit. The leaders are not going to tell you something that will kill you. I am not saying that rebuke does not hurt. However, your leader's correction should make you want to seek God the more for your deliverance. The Word of God teaches that "if you confess with thy mouth and believe in thine heart, thy will be saved." It also teaches that "those that name the name of Christ, depart from iniquity." No saint or believer should be angry with his or her leader for a long period of time for correction, especially if the leader is rebuking you for sin. Your leader is placed over you to watch over your soul, to keep you covered from dangers seen and unseen. Respect that God is in them, and God will pour out unexpected blessings upon you. Be blessed in the Lord. Obey leadership and deliver your soul.

As for that faithful person of God, Satan is coming after your dedication. Your faith will be shaken. Your loyalty will be shaken. Your obedience will be shaken. If you desire a true relationship with God, your love will be shaken. Why? Because Satan knows he has but a short time. But God is faithful, and he is just toward his people.

We are witnessing and receiving the promises of God in the ministry. God spoke and declared that the ministry will not go down. God has the apostle and prophetess covered. We know and stand on the Word of God. Isaiah 54:17 states, "No weapon formed against thee shall prosper and every tongue that should rise up, in judgment thou shall condemn, this is the heritage of your people." Furthermore, Jeremiah 29:11 reads, "I know the thoughts that I think towards thee, thoughts of good and not evil to give you an expected end."

You see the glory now because a price was paid for the anointing on the apostle's and prophetess's lives. Their faiths were tested because God said he would fill the house. However, they had to experience faithful members leave the ministry. In addition, they had to endure financial hardship. Furthermore, the leaders confronted with forces from hell. There were times they desired to walk away and relocate due to people's rebellion and disobedience. Their obedience was tested in difficult moments when they had to keep silent, when everyone around them was low-rating and persecuting them without a cause. The leaders were not allowed to defend themselves. The apostle and the prophetess were forced to suffer for Christ's sake.

Love was tested also. God required them to love and receive the enemies that caused them hardships. The leaders had to love and forgive those who lied and plotted against the ministry.

Oftentimes, God would have the apostle and prophetess pray for and heal them. "Love and kindness have I drawn thee," said the Lord.

Pastors and bishops, we are in perilous times, and God has placed judgment on the church. It is time to bring your house in order and call a solemn assembly. Even as Paul encouraged Timothy in the Gospel, we encourage you to preach the Gospel of Jesus. There is one blood, one faith, and one baptism. God said that no longer will he shake the earth but heaven also, and only the Kingdom would remain.

Chapter 8

The Process

Like many other major prophets of the Bible, Prophetess White is misunderstood. God allows her to suffer shame in the public's eye. Her life is an open book. "It is good for me that I have been afflicted; that I might learn thy statutes" as stated in Psalm 119:71. David was afflicted by God and learned how to wait for his promises.

Many may admire the woman who walk with God. Prophetess White has gone through a process for the anointing. God placed a special anointing in her for nations of people. God processed her in his own timing, and he released Prophetess White into her destiny. Through this process, the prophetess often told us that no matter what she experienced in her trials, she would give God the glory.

God is not slack concerning his promises. He is waiting on you. God moves in his own timing, and I had to learn how to operate in the timing of God. Being in the time of the Lord is so important, people of God. Once I learned how to wait patiently on God, things began to fall in place. Yes, opposition came, and it only made me trust God the more. I found myself thanking God for my enemies. I found myself rejoicing and worshiping God when my back was against the wall. The timing of the Lord is not like ours.

One day with the Lord is like a thousand years. To us, it seems like God is never going to move or fulfill his promises. We forget that our lives can be changed in a moment's time with God. The Bible teaches us not to be anxious for anything. We often read that patience is a virtue. It seems we forget our teaching when a trial hits. Always remember, people of God, that great trials become God's blessings.

Prophetess Personal Testimony

I had to wait over ten years to receive all that God had promised me. It was 1991 when God showed me my destiny. All I knew God was going to raise me up to lead a people. I did not obey God to fullness. God had to process me. He placed me in the woods and processed me. He killed White.

Man does not get the glory for the anointing on my life. God saved me back in the early eighties, and I made up my mind. For God I will live, and for God I will die. I realized before God took me to the woods for over nine years that God would be my life. I had such a hunger and thirst for God. I thought at times that I was losing my mind. I wanted more of God. The more I sought God, the more he revealed himself unto me the latter days of his coming. God began to raise me up in the midst of a heathen nation of people. He placed a divine word in my belly for such a time as this. I did not know at that time that God would cause me to lead a people. I did not know that God himself would be my schoolmaster. People of God, the visions, dreams, and prophecies came one after the other. I felt like I was not worthy of such a heavy task. But it was through much fasting, praying, and studying the Word that God revealed himself to me. I can't explain the assignment in its entirety because man would not understand. The places I have walked in and the avenues my feet have treaded, man would not believe. I found myself wanting nothing but Jesus. I did not ask to be raised. All I ever wanted was to please him. People, let me tell you something that is so, key. All God really wanted was somebody he could trust. All God ever desired was a vessel that will not sell out, deny themselves for the Kingdom. Truly God is no respect of person; he just wants a willing vessel to pour himself in.

The authority I walk in came through me being obedient and faithful to God, and the leaders he placed over me. My gift is very rare, and it carries a heavy burden. Never once did I ask for this. It has not been easy to carry Jesus in a place where Jesus is not wanted. Many times I just wanted to lay down this assignment, but God strengthened me. God gave me supernatural strength to not only carry the vision, but also he allowed me to birth nations of people that I never met nor laid eyes upon. I have just one thing to leave with you. If God ever gave you a vision, dream, task, and or assignment, just know he will perform that which he has promised you. Stay focused no matter what state you may find yourself in. Seek God in the midst of your troubles, and he will see you through.

Chapter 9

Someone Will Pick You Up in the Spirit

Your gift will make room for you. The Bible also teaches that promotion does not come from the east or from the west or from the south. We live in a competitive world. It is sad to see that the body of Christ has become just as competitive. The Bible teaches in the book of Corinthians that there are many gifts but one spirit. It also teaches that many are called, but few are chosen. With all the souls in the world, the body of Christ seems to fight over major and minor platforms to preach on. No one wants to roll up his or her sleeves to work in the highways and hedges anymore. "There is no money in it," we say. One thing I learned from the apostle and prophetess at FFC Ministries International is that if there is no process, there is no glory. I have learned that in order for God to release the promises, I had to be broken. I had to go through an hour of suffering. My faith had to be tested on many levels. I watched the apostle and prophetess as God raised them up to lead nations of people. One thing I can say is that they have never bragged on themselves. They have always given God the glory for what he is doing in the ministry. Never once had the apostle and prophetess boasted in their flesh when God used them. Many prophets, bishops, evangelists, and apostles have always picked them up in the Holy Ghost. I have also learned that you do not have to tear someone else down to build yourself up. They have always led humble and submissive lives. The leaders of the FFC ministry taught the members how to serve other people's ministry. Through this teaching, God has established them in the midst of notable ministers. The Bible teaches us that we should always esteem another man higher than ourselves. Even John the Baptist said to his disciples, "I must decrease because he must increase." He spoke those words because he recognized that he was not the people's savior. He only came to bear witness to Jesus, that Jesus is the son of God. This same principle is taught today. We, as members and supporters of ministry, should be the forerunners for our leaders. Furthermore, when our leaders show up on the scene, we should humble ourselves before them. I must write this because God has let me know beforehand that many major prophets and more will read this book. Even though you have a great ministry and God is using you mightily, God is going to give you the love and respect for the anointing that operates in Apostle Richard's and Prophetess Lucinda's life. Also, God will honor and increase you for supporting the ministry as they deliver a saving word to God's people. If you want the favor of God to rest in your life, support with your prayers as well as your finances. Sew into the ministry and watch God move for you in new ways. The anointing that rests on the apostle and prophetess speaks for itself. I encourage you to esteem the anointing in the prophetess and the apostle higher than yourself and watch God move.

I came to realize that if God be with you, he will fight for you. Not only will God fight for you, he will place people in your life to sustain you. Even as the widow sustained Elijah, God has sent people to the ministry to sustain the apostle and the prophetess. As the leaders of God go before him in prayer and supplication, God is allowing other noble people in other areas to pick up their spirit.

I can remember in 2004 when God began to break tradition off the ministry. People would call the apostle and prophetess and tell them what God was going to do through them in the last days. Prophets from all over the world called and encouraged the man and woman of God to stay focused on the vision. Also, these particular prophets were very accurate with the Word of God. This is one of the words that were stated, "That the FFC and

LWM ministries would excel all the major ministries, which are already in operation."

Thinking back on the promises that God gave the leaders of the FFC Ministries International, God promised that he will place people in the ministry from all over the world, and these people shall be a pillar for the ministry. They will have a mind to work ministry and be obedient to leadership. God's promise is to make their name great in the earth and in heaven. Most of all, no man would get the glory for what has taken place within the ministry. We testify! God is not a man that he should lie, neither is he the son of man that he should repent.

Chapter 10

The Passover

There is a twofold message revealed in the Bible. I discovered that great betrayal, manipulation, and deceit all played significant roles. There were unexpected twists and suspense in this chapter. But in the end, I truly understood why God allowed these events to take place. Jesus is our "Passover" because he brings us consolation in our time of need. He strengthens our spirit and empowers us to stand in the midst of opposition. Jesus continues to deliver us from our bondage and captivated state.

Think about the first Passover and how the Israelites cried unto God. It took nine plagues and the death of Pharaoh's son before they were allowed to leave Egypt. Then Pharaoh's army pursued them, and God made a way of escape. Now the Jews celebrate this event because God brought them out with a strong hand. When studying what took place in the apostles' era, I discovered some profound situations that occurred. Jesus knew that his time had arrived to be crucified. However, those that were close to him were blind, or they completely ignored the Words of God. Probably, they had convinced each other that Jesus is God, and no one can harm him. Were the disciples too afraid to stand up for what they believed? We know that they all forsook him. I am wondering about what truly took place. Jesus knew their thoughts and actions. He warned the disciples about his death.

Then I considered the scribes and the high priest. These individuals knew the law and why it was important for someone to be released and crucified. They understood the will of God in part but refused to acknowledge Jesus as the son of God. The high priest understood that blood must be shed for the sin of the people. "Caiaphas was he, which gave counsel to the Jews." He stated, "It was expedient that one man should die for the people" (John 18:14). Caiaphas had received the revelation from the beginning of time. God spoke to Moses to instruct the Israelites to kill a lamb and spread blood on the doorpost and lintels. In the event that death comes, it will see the blood and would pass over the house. This is how Israel escaped from Pharaoh, because of the blood.

Now Jesus is about to be offered up for the sins of the people. You must understand, during the Feast of the Passover, the Jews would release someone from prison and someone would be killed. At this time, we learn about Barabbas, the murderer. I believe Caiaphas knew that a murderer could not die for the sins of the people. This is why Jesus came on the scene to redeem mankind back to God. It took the blood of Jesus to save the world. Lamb's blood could not wash away our sins. I look back and realize that the first Passover was symbolic to Jesus's crucifixion. God had Barabbas in mind on that day. He wanted to save the Jews and Gentiles as well.

I am grateful because no other man was qualified to redeem my soul back to God. We know that Jesus rose after these events. Now we celebrate Jesus's death, burial, and resurrection. I can now ask what I will in Jesus's name.

God is not like man. If we read and meditate on God's Word, he will bring us out. They all were forgiven on that day. Judas's betrayal was forgiven; he had a chance to receive Jesus. The Jews were forgiven and had a chance to receive Jesus. Peter's and the other disciples' denial were forgiven. And now we have an opportunity to receive his spirit.

It is imperative to remember the cross and how Jesus granted us grace and mercy. Jesus said, "If any man would follow me, he first must deny himself." John 1:12 and 14 states, "The word was made flesh and we beheld his glory, as many have received Him, he gave them power to become the sons of God."

The revelation behind the Passover is that God delivered them, and the Israelites received a great blessing. They had an abundance of gold, silver, cattle, and grain. They received their inheritance. Everything that they labored for while in Egypt was given back a hundredfold. Listen, people, God is about to bring you out of your circumstances and hardships. You have been held back too long. It is time to cry out, travail before the Lord until he comes through on our behalf.

In the book Matthew 16:13-19, Jesus asked them, "Whom do men say that I the son man am? Peter answered and said, Thou art the Christ, the son of the Living God. Jesus said, Thou art Peter and upon this rock I will build my church and the gates of hell shall not prevail against it. And I will give unto thee the keys of the kingdom of heaven: and whatsoever thou shalt bind on earth shalt be bind in heaven and whatsoever thou shalt loose on earth shall be loosed in heaven." Jesus does this action just before they entered Jerusalem, where the Jews were preparing for the Passover. Jesus reminds the disciples that he must be offered up.

What about now? Jesus is our Passover. Jesus is breaking the chains of death and spiritual blindness. When he hung on the cross for you and me, he redeemed man back to God. Jesus encouraged them in the book of John 14-17 about his departure. Jesus told the disciples, "I must go away to prepare a place for you. And because I go unto the father, you can ask what you will, and it will be given to you by my father." He also said, "I will send the comforter to you, and he will lead and guide you." The comforter is the Holy Ghost. Jesus's death, burial, and resurrection is our spiritual Passover, and now we have fellowship with God. This is why he is celebrated.

Chapter 11

The Release

Go Ye to the Gentiles

Apostle Richard White has entered and operated in the Pastoral and Overseer Office of the FFC International, and God has released the prophetess to travel and do God's work. Many doors are opening for the woman of God to preach the Gospel across the globe. Prophetess White has a divine assignment from God. She is to preach deliverance to a dying generation. As the prophetess to the nations, Prophetess Lucinda is to restore order to the body of Christ. In addition, she intercedes for the governmental system in prayer and fasting. Many will look to her for guidance and leadership. Just as God placed John the Baptist in the wilderness to be a forerunner for Christ, he caused Apostle Richard and prophetess Lucinda White to reside on the back side of the desert for such a time as this. The world is seeking for the next leader. We need someone that will provide, love, and guide during these dark days. Thank God for our presidents, governors, senators, entertainers, professional athletes, philosophers, and educators, but their wisdom and expertise cannot bring restoration to our economy, community, families, individual hearts, or the human spirit. In this hour, we must turn to God for the answers. The next revolution is coming through the people of God. It is time to look to Jesus like never before. Psalm 121:1-2 tells me to "look unto the hills from which cometh my help; my help cometh from the Lord, the maker and creator of heaven and earth." It is in him that we live, move, and have our being. America needs a revival from the White House to the drug house and from the school house to the church house. A revival is coming to the four corners of the earth, which shall cause us to cry out to God one more time. We are living in the hour where people are looking for signs from heaven to warn them of the second coming of Christ. This generation cannot understand the signs of the time. God is speaking like never before, but no one has an ear or eye to hear what the spirit is saying.

The body of Christ has entered into an hour where the pastors, bishops, and leaders must go after the harvest, for the harvest is ripe and labors are few. A trumpet has been sounding in the spirit for some time now. He that has an ear let him hear what the spirit is saying unto the church.

It is time for lay members to mature and stand on your own. If you have been saved for five years or more, you should be able to pray for yourself and fight your own battles. We, as members, have taken our leaders for granted. The congregation has been disrespecting and prostituting the pastor's anointing. I am guilty of this as well. However, God sent me a wake-up call. I began to see when God opened my eyes. I was hearing the Word, but I did not allow the Word to take root. Since the Word was not taking root in my spirit, I was stagnated, and true deliverance did not take place in my heart. I repented and asked God to teach me how to receive the Word regardless if it hurt my flesh or not. When I cried out to God, he took me in the scriptures and showed me the error of my ways.

Isaiah 65:1-3 states, "I am sought of them that asked not for me; I am found of them that sought me not: I said, behold me, behold me, unto a nation that was not called by my name. I have spread out my hands all the day unto a rebellious people, which walketh in a way that was not good, after their own thoughts; A people that provoketh me to anger continually to my face; that sacrificeth in gardens, and burneth incense upon altars of brick." I repented for not loving God the way I was testifying that I loved him. When I read this scripture, I meditated on it day and night because I wanted the love of God on the inside. I was in church and not the Kingdom of God. I had fellowship with God and not a relationship. I still held unforgiveness in my heart and possessed a prideful spirit. I judged people before I really knew them. Anger and hurt held me captive, and I was unable to truly trust God the way I needed to. But God had mercy on my soul. I thank him for the love that he placed inside of my leaders. They loved me enough to preach and live the Word of God before me and the society. I now understand the importance of showing the real love of God. The body of Christ as a whole must exemplify the love of God in our daily lives.

This is why Isaiah preached this message. Isaiah realized that hypocrisy was killing the Israelites. Israel worshipped other gods more than they worshipped the true and living God. After God delivered them out of bondage and brought them into the promised land, Israel disobeyed his commands. We know this is the year of release, and the horn of plenty is already sounding; however, it is not time to be at ease, take vacations, or be overtaken by prosperity. When God released the supernatural blessings in our lives, we must stay on our faces, crying out to him the more. Isaiah preached in the chapter 56 about how Israel and Judah turned away from God and began to do what other nations were doing. They worshipped idol gods, images, creatures but still desired to be called by Jesus's name. These same spirits are in the earth today, and many of us are being overtaken by them. Iniquity and hypocrisy are their names. God is saying to turn back to him. God's judgment is about to come upon us if we don't get back to fasting, praying, and studying the Word. We must return back to God. People of God, we cannot continue to operate in our gifts and not have a real relationship with God. We must get delivered from lust, fornication, backbiting, unforgiveness, and pride. We are standing in the way of sinners that desire to be saved. The spirit of Ananias and Sapphira has been loosed in the earth, and judgment is coming to those that refuse to turn away from sin. This generation of people is exhibiting the same behavior as Israel. Israel disobeyed and persecuted the prophets because the people did not want to walk in the statutes of God. I am looking across the globe at the church and seeing the pastors, bishops, and others fall into sin. But God will have voices in the earth that is going to cry out against the wickedness in the people. God will have prophets compelling the people to return back to him. Destruction is in the land, and it is because of God's people refusing to repent. That is why God is about to do a switch in the earth.

He is about to go to the Gentiles. In the Bible days, the Gentiles were people that were not associated with the Israelites. According to history, the Gentiles were nations not associated with the Jews. The Jewish race defined Gentile as a foreigner or an alien. Also any nation of people that did not serve the true living God but worshiped idols and false gods were considered Gentiles. In the beginning, God found favor in the Israelites and entered into a covenant agreement with them. Genesis 12 records the covenant agreement between God and Abraham. God instructed Abraham (Abram) to leave his native country and journey to a land that he would show him. God promised Abraham that he would make Abraham's name great and make Abraham a great nation. The covenant guaranteed that all nations would be blessed through Abraham's seed (Gen. 12:1-5). Therefore, in our day, the Gentiles are the gamblers, drug dealers, entertainers, gang leaders, and others that do not have dealings with the church society. God is going after those people that do not fellowship in any form of religious practices. God is about to put his spirit within them, and they are going to represent the Kingdom of God. Joel 2:28 and Acts 2:17 state, "In the last days I will pour out my Spirit and your sons and daughters shall prophesy and your old men shall see vision and your young men shall dream dreams and upon my handmaidens and servants shall I pour it out." John 10:16 and 27 mentions, "I have other sheep, which are not of this fold: them also I must bring, and they shall hear my voice; and there shall be one fold and one shepherd. My sheep knows my voice and a stranger they will not follow."

God is tired of the complainers, the haters of truth, and the false teachings of religion. God is a spirit, and those that worship him must worship in spirit and in truth. I'm reminded of Joshua and how he stood in the midst of his generation and declared, "For me and my house, we are going to serve the Lord." O my God, body of Christ, wake up! The devil is trying to kill out the Joshua generation. The last-hour church that will pave the way for coming of our Lord Jesus Christ is about to come on the scene. The Joshua generation is coming forth with power and authority. This generation won't have on a suit. This generation will not be concerned with organizations and dominations. They will minister a "thus sayeth the Lord" message, which shall bring conviction within the hearts of man.

The release is a prophet movement that is taking place now in the earth. It is very important to stay in prayer and study the Word of God. God is releasing an anointing of Elijah and Moses on the people. But if you are not in the right place with God, you are going to miss the move of God. We must mature in the Word now. We cannot be shaken because people do not like our ministry. God is looking for some warriors. God said that he will make our feet like hind feet and teach our hands to war. Moses and Elijah both worked miracles and great signs and wonders. They also possessed the true power of God.

> But there were false prophets also among the people, even as there shall be false teachers among you, who privily shall bring in damnable heresies, even denying the Lord that bought them, and bring upon themselves swift destruction. (2 Pet. 2:1)

Moses and Elijah were faced with battling false prophets and magicians that formed illusions similar to the work of God. In this hour, false prophets are going to be operating in signs and wonders just like the church. Second Thessalonians 2:7-10 states, "For the mystery of iniquity doth already work: only he who now letteth will let, until he be taken out of the way. And then shall that Wicked be revealed, whom the Lord shall consume with the spirit of his mouth, and shall destroy with the brightness of his coming: Even him, whose coming is after the working of Satan with all power and signs and lying wonders, And with all deceivableness of unrighteousness in them that perish; because they received not the love of the truth, that they might be saved."

Now as Jannes and Jambres withstood Moses, so do these also resist the truth: men of corrupt minds, reprobate concerning the faith. But they shall not proceed no further: for their folly shall be manifest unto all men, as their's also was. (2 Tim. 3:8-9)

God is going to anoint us to stand and endure the persecution and hardships that is about to be released in the earth. God is going hide his people. In the midst of the trouble, you got to know who God is.

Chapter 12

Words from the Apostle

As the pastor for the Firebrands for Christ Ministries International, apostle Richard White has a testimony of his own to share with the world. "Being married to a great woman of God has been a joy for me. Through all our hard times, God has made us one. No devil will come between us," he would often tell us in the ministry.

I became the pastor, and it was a switch. Pastor Lucinda White who has been pastor of FFC from the start up to October 1999 got it off the ground. She is my beautiful wife and prophetess to the nation, but on May 14, 2006, God released her to a greater platform to go the nation, not only to the USA, but also to Africa, India, unto the four corners of the earth. So you see, I did not ask for this office or to preach. The Lord ordained me to be what I am. Like Jeremiah stated in 1:5, I did not call myself, but the Lord ordained me to do what I am about to do. The Lord speaks to me as he did Moses in the book of Numbers 12:8. Revelation 12:2 states, "Jesus Christ paid the price at Calvary's cross over two thousand years ago, He suffered and blood came running down the cross." In 1 Corinthians 1:26-29, Paul stated that "for ye see your calling brethren how that not many wise men often the flesh not many mighty, not many noble one called. But God had chosen the foolish of this world to confound the wise, and God has chosen the weak things of the world to confound the things which are mighty, No flesh should glory in his presence." Even as David was anointed in the midst of his brethren, so am I the least in my family, but God be the glory. It was David's faith and obedience to God, which set him up for the throne. Hebrews 5:8 states, "Though He [Christ] was a son, yet He learned obedience by the things which He suffered." *Behind the Glory* is a story of our ministry. And this ministry, in years later, shall tell a great story from beginning to end.

I have seen God do that which is impossible for man. Since I became pastor of the FFC Ministries International, I have taken limits off God. Why? Because I can have just what God's Word say I can have. If God be for me, he is more than the whole world against me. Truly, greater is he that is on the inside than he that is in the world. We, as the children of God, shall receive an inheritance. There are some promises that God has given, and the body of Christ is getting ready to take their rightful place in the earth.

> The kingdom of heaven suffereth violence, violence take it by force. (Matt. 11:12)

I don't know about you. But I am taking everything that I lost over the years because of ignorance. I am taking back those things that which were stolen from me. The devil, Satan, has to return all my stuff back—double. I am going after God now like never before. I believe God's Word for what it says. He said that his people will possess the land, then I am going to possess it. It is "not by might nor by power, but by my Spirit says the Lord." We wrestle not against flesh and blood but against principalities, powers, and wickedness in high places. I truly understand my warfare. My fight is not with my brother and my sister. It is with Satan, the adversary, that tells me I cannot have what God promised me. We all have read about the promises of God in Deuteronomy 28, but I am tired of the Word being of none effect in my life. God is not a man that he should lie, neither the son of man that he should repent. Isaiah 55 states that "He sent forth his word into the earth and it accomplished that which he sent out to do and will not return void."

I can ask what I will if I live right and keep his commandments. I can seek, and I shall find. Knock and it shall be opened unto you.

We are living in the greatest times now. The heavens are opened, and I am pulling down my blessings from God. I am calling things though they are not as though they were. We are sitting under an opened heaven, and God is pouring out new mercies, new blessings, new miracles, new breakthroughs, and new chances every day. Truly, I am leaving the dark days behind. I press toward the prize of a higher calling, which is in Christ Jesus. No longer will I set limits on what God can do. He came that I might have life and live more abundantly. Where is the God of Elijah? Where is the God of Elijah? I am not looking for fire to fall from heaven. I am looking for the people of God to believe him and his Word. The Word has power. Speak the Word and the Word only. I speak life to every dead issue that is your life today. If you can only believe, people of God. Even as Jesus called Lazarus forth, I call you out of your dead situations. I command you to live and not die to declare the works of the Lord. I encourage you today to get up from the dead state that you are in. Why die when you can live? There is hope for you. You don't have to wait until someone comes by to pray for you. Take the Word of God and apply it to your life. Read and believe God for what his tells us. If you can only believe the Word, then God can move for you. Let God speak to your circumstances. When God saved me, I did not fully understand the Word or his ways. My wife could do so many things in the Word through her faith. I did not know Matthew from John, but look at me now. God has given the knowledge and understanding of his Word. I have seen God move in my own life enough to encourage you. If you get out of yourself and what you feel is right, then God can move for you. Too many times we want what we want but don't want the sacrifice that comes. But God is getting ready to bless his people. I can't stress this enough. It does not take God long to bless us. We must learn how to position ourselves and wait on God. Since I have been pastor, my outlook has change concerning my walk with God. I have found myself pushing past what I see or feel. Every time I press my way through something, God meets me the more. I allowed God to process me. I took a death walk with God. I don't have a degree from a prestigious university or college. All I have is the Holy Ghost. I have found out that God is not concerned with my knowledge and wisdom. That does not move him. What does move God is my obedience and faith. I can decree a thing, and God will honor it. In 2004, I started saying that I was a millionaire. In 2005, I said that I was a billionaire. Now I decree and proclaim that I am a trillionaire. I have been faithful over a few things, and God truly has made me ruler over many. He has brought me from the pit to the palace. He has performed his promises unto me and my wife. I am not worthy of the blessings, but it was my faithfulness down through the years that brought me to my wealthy place.

About the Author

I can do nothing without God. It is in him that I live and move and have my being. I have committed my works unto the Lord, and my thoughts have been established. Since my birth into the Kingdom of God, I have learned how to forgive, love unconditionally, be compassionate, faithful, and obedient and walk in humility. I am aspiring to be more like my Lord and Savior, Jesus. As the author of *Behind the Glory*, I understand the challenges in which Christian writers face when producing a prophetic word to the world. I would not take anything for the lessons learned and the difficult test that I had to take. Over the years, God has proven me. I paid a price to be the author of this book.

I have two degrees from Alabama Agricultural and Mechanical University, and I am in the process of starting law school. I have traveled on mission trips to Africa. I have traveled to many states within the United States. Also, I had many rewarding jobs and internships. But none of these things can compare to this experience of completing my first book.